What Is Prana?

Theosophical Publishing Society

Kessinger Publishing's Rare Reprints

Thousands of Scarce and Hard-to-Find Books on These and other Subjects!

- Americana
- Ancient Mysteries
- Animals
- Anthropology
- Architecture
- Arts
- Astrology
- Bibliographies
- Biographies & Memoirs
- Body, Mind & Spirit
- Business & Investing
- Children & Young Adult
- Collectibles
- Comparative Religions
- Crafts & Hobbies
- Earth Sciences
- Education
- Ephemera
- Fiction
- Folklore
- Geography
- Health & Diet
- History
- Hobbies & Leisure
- Humor
- Illustrated Books
- Language & Culture
- Law
- Life Sciences
- Literature
- Medicine & Pharmacy
- Metaphysical
- Music
- Mystery & Crime
- Mythology
- Natural History
- Outdoor & Nature
- Philosophy
- Poetry
- Political Science
- Science
- Psychiatry & Psychology
- Reference
- Religion & Spiritualism
- Rhetoric
- Sacred Books
- Science Fiction
- Science & Technology
- Self-Help
- Social Sciences
- Symbolism
- Theatre & Drama
- Theology
- Travel & Explorations
- War & Military
- Women
- Yoga
- *Plus Much More!*

**We kindly invite you to view our catalog list at:
http://www.kessinger.net**

THIS ARTICLE WAS EXTRACTED FROM THE BOOK:

Theosophical Siftings: A Collection of Essays

BY THIS AUTHOR:

Theosophical Publishing Society

ISBN 076612990X

READ MORE ABOUT THE BOOK AT OUR WEB SITE:

http://www.kessinger.net

OR ORDER THE COMPLETE
BOOK FROM YOUR FAVORITE STORE

ISBN 076612990X

Because this article has been extracted from a parent book, it may have non-pertinent text at the beginning or end of it.

WHAT IS PRANA?

PRANA is life, and we at once inquire whether in essence it belongs to the spiritual or physical worlds. But absolutely it cannot be assigned to either. There are not several kinds of life; there is only one kind; but several kinds of creatures have it. Life is meta-everything, metaphysical and meta-spiritual. The crystal has life, for it grows; the plant has life, for it grows, moves, and feels; the animal has life, for it does all these and has conscious desires; mind has life, for it thinks; spirit has life, for it creates. Each of the seven principles of man has life, for each works according to its fashion. Life is comparable to one moon falling upon a thousand ripples, and creating thereon a semblance of a thousand moons. But really the Universe is only one infinite life, and it seems multitudinous during its active periods because of the multitudinous creatures that have it. Some, because they are low, exhibit it in its low aspects, such as physical force; and the highest god in Cosmos, because he is high, exhibits it in its highest aspect. But it is greater in its as yet unmanifested aspects and potencies than any of the creatures who live in it, reflect it, and assimilate ever more and more of it. Greater than all lives and behind them stands life, the life because of which they live. Here is the secret of evolution, because it is this life, infinite in its unrevealed possibilities, infinite in surface and depth, that is always consciously struggling to make its creatures reveal it more fully, to make the stone arise into vegetation, to make the vegetable consciously desire, to make the animal think, to raise man into spirituality; all the way up it is trying to make its creatures exhibit more and more of it, to realise itself in them. In its infinity it can never be known, but if we take a line from the stone to ourselves, and from ourselves to Those whom we know as Masters, and note how from step to step ever greater powers and functions come into play, and how consciousness grows ever wider and deeper, and then try and shoot the line onwards to infinity, the attempt will help us into a kind of awe; for unless we can conceive the infinite, *the life* is beyond all ken, although we *are* it on every plane of our being. Evolution is the gradual dissolving of the limits that bind the life, for though we give up physical life, the life of longing remains; though we give up longing, thought remains; though we suspend thought, egoism remains; though we transcend egoism, there is consciousness greater than and freed from that, for egoism is limitation. Philosophically and theoretically we can go one step higher, for even consciousness in any form in which we know it is limited, and we are trying to feel after the unlimited. We can call the one life Jiva, the animator, the motion, the activity of the seven planes. Every student of Theosophy knows what are the seven human principles, or the seven aspects in which we have to study man and the universe. We know that prana or vitality is counted as one of the seven which are given to the beginner to help his study. But if we are right in saying that the universe is only *one* life, life or vitality belongs equally to all the seven principles, since if they had not life they would not *be*. Life is the ocean of being in which all the principles float; therefore prana or life is the same as Jiva, and it is not one of the seven principles, but the source of them all, and only knowable because it manifests itself in them, and increasingly as we go up the list. Let us leave it out in our enumeration, for if we put it in, it becomes necessary to include the higher and lower Manas under one head. *We are* the lower Manas, the last attribute of the monad or unit of life which has trailed its slow way up through the kingdoms of nature to the thinking human stage; the higher Manas is Prometheus, Krishna, the guide and inspirer. The principles may therefore, for purposes of study, be best arranged thus:—

(1) Atma.
(2) Buddhi.
(3) Buddhi-Manas.
(4) Kama-Manas.
(5) Kama.
(6) Linga Sharira : astral body.
(7) Sthula Sharira : physical body.

All these seven being manifestations of life, Jiva, in different kinds and degrees. The lowest plane, the physical, is the densest, and therefore allows fewest of the potencies of life to shine through it, those namely that we call physical and chemical forces. Through this plane the universal life exhibits itself as the attraction and repulsion of molecules, light, heat, sound, electricity, etc. Confining our study to man, all these forces are exhibited by the gross fabric of his body, whether *he* is conscious or unconscious, and whether *it* is " dead " or " living ".

On the next plane, the astral, matter is very much finer, and the life, besides exhibiting the foregoing properties, exhibits the attributes of physical or physiological vitality. Vitality, or prana, is a group of forces diffused throughout the astral body, as the astral body is diffused throughout the physical. It is a special form of force, acting through the astral body on to the physical. Death is the departure of it; and though the physical and chemical forces act just as well in the body after death as during life, during life they are *under the control of vitality*, and compelled so to comport themselves as to preserve and not destroy the body. Materialistic science, or physiology, denies the existence of this force, and asserts that bodily life is *only* physical and chemical activity. Law is definable as "an observed relationship between phenomena", and *on the plane* of the phenomena this is all that can be postulated of it, but on its own plane above the phenomena law is an entity, though metaphysical. Prana, so far as the plane accessible to the objective physiologist is concerned, is nothing but that relationship between the bodily physical forces or processes that makes for bodily conservation. But on its own plane, accessible only to the occultist (thus far) it is an entity, and its withdrawal, necessitating loss of co-operatively constructive activity of the forces beneath it, is death. In a subsequent paper I hope to go into the *process* of the directive activity, but in this place the above statement will do, and we will pass to the other planes.

Just as the physical and chemical forces on the bodily plane are under the control of vitality or prana on the astral plane, so the pranic group in their turn are under the control of Kama, the animal desire—consciousness, on the Kamic plane. On this Kamic plane, Jiva, the all-potential life, is enabled through the still finer matter of Kama Rupa to display another, a third plane, of attributes. Each of the seven human principles may be regarded as a plane of substance (the term *matter* may be used of the four lower planes) a rupa, a body. Matter is that which limits the manifestations of Jiva, and since as we go up the scale of the human principles the state of matter gets finer, more subtle, more *subjective*, complexer, so is Jiva increasingly able to manifest through them its higher potencies and qualities. On the physical and astral planes it shows itself respectively as force and vitality. On the plane of Kama Rupa it is conscious animal desire, hunger, lust, animal volition; desire leading to activity. These activities need vitality or prana to carry them out, and vitality in its turn needs the physico-chemical forces to keep together the body it works in. Hence Kama on the Kama Rupic plane uses and controls prana on the astral plane, which in its turn uses and controls the forces of the physical plane.

Again, Kama tends with the evolution of humanity to pass under the control of the lower Manas. The rupa of the lower Manas is substantive, a grade finer than the rupa of Kama. Through the substantive basis of the lower Manas, the One Life, Jiva, is enabled to exhibit that aspect of itself which we call mind, and as we ascend the steps of being, mind and reason as a force tend more and more to control desire or the lusts, as desire uses vitality and vitality force.

Ascending yet another plane of substance, we reach the higher Manas:

above this Buddhi, and lastly Atma. Through these higher principles, the Jiva is rather to be regarded as manifesting grades of consciousness than force, just as through the lower three it manifests rather force than consciousness. But this is rather a convenient statement than the actual fact; the distinction is for purposes of study, and the lower Manas which we know as " I " combines the potentiality of all the others. In these three higher states we see three manifestations of one all-pervading consciousness, the threefold mind in nature. Atma is the memory of the Universe, and the plan to which nature is moulding itself in its evolution; when nature *has* moulded itself thereto, Atma becomes memory. In Buddhi the world-consciousness becomes something like what the Christian thinks of as the omnipresent God, the self-conscious force of nature; while in the higher Manas this world-self has become the permanent egos or selves of men, each expressing and carrying out a bit of the whole, just as each musician in an orchestra contributes his special quality of instrumental effect to the whole result of tone. Thus, in brief, does the one great, inconceivably great life breathe through creation. Supra-conscious life on the highest plane, it becomes self-conscious life on the next, human individual self-consciousness on the next, rational mind on the next, desire in matter on the next, physical life on the next, and force on the last. Let us examine the sequence from above downward.

1. Atma.—The programme of the Universe in its evolution from first to last; the pre-existing plan of what will be, and the memory of what has been, as they exist in that all-present cosmic mind.

2. Buddhi.—The same mind as a self-conscious creative actor; "God", as a pantheistic Christian would call it.

3. The same mind reflected in the mind of man; broken up into rays of which every man is illuminated by one, the higher Manas.

These three are the three aspects or functions of the Universal Mind, which itself exists in the one life and manifests that life after these three fashions. As pointed out at first, there are not many lives in the Universe, but one life possessed by many creatures; a life so great and deep that no creature can live it fully or manifest it fully. Each has life after one or many fashions, but none has it after all fashions. There are, for ever, heights of life that no conscious mind of any grade can show forth or think out as yet.

Therefore, through the universal mind we may say that the Jiva shines forth as creative intention, designing thought, and action from self-consciousness. And always the universal minds of future universal dramas of evolution will intend, design, and create, after grander and grander fashions.

Thus far we have succeeded in a measure in realising that each of the grades of life in the universe and man commands the grade below. Atma is the pattern or law after which Buddhi or Mahat the creator (" God ") works; whose instruments are the divine egos of men, the higher Manas. egos which have other work than that which we recognise in ourselves, The lower Manas of men is increasingly under the sway of the higher (conscience), and this lower, the thinking self is increasingly the ruler of Kama, lust for sensation. Kama is inert without the astral qualities of sensation and vitality, whilst vitality (prana) is the soul of the bodily forces.

Let us see what practical bearings upon our lives has this view of one omnipresent life. First then, it prompts us to unselfishness, for we are all responsible for the condition of each other. It is often asked of Theosophists to what real end are their speculations and subtleties. No one can dwell long upon a thought, without its presently becoming a basis of action. Very well, the conception upon which we are now dwelling is this. Before evolution began, and before men and worlds were in being, one soul breathed in the emptiness, and it was this soul which moved into evolution according to a plan of its own. And in pursuit of that plan it shot itself out into the rays we call men, a duality in consciousness of the material and the spiritual. All men follow diverse paths and go through diverse pains and rough places, that this soul *in them* may perfect itself in all experiences. And since all men were once lost in the unity of that soul which together they composed (for it is not a thing distinct from them) all men, like the members of a committee, are alike responsible for the doings of the whole. The doings and plan of the whole comprise the fractionation of the whole into units, and for each of these the whole or the collectivity of all is responsible. And in the same way as the American said he had rheumatism in his brother, we can truly say we have sin in our brother and misery. It is this unconscious knowledge that it is we who are miserable in him that leads us to relieve his misery. I relieve misery to relieve *my* misery at seeing it. I am miserable at seeing want, because I in that other man am in want. There is no other explanation of charity and there are few who have not at one time or another time done a charity. Some would reduce it all to selfishness, saying that we only relieve pain to relieve our own pain at seeing it. Precisely true. We have widened our interests till they include others. We are in pain at the pain of another. To that extent we do not distinguish between ourselves and him, because at bottom there is no such distinction. Humanity is one Self. At the beginning it was one; it now seems many, but at the end when the minds of men are tuned together (a process already indicated by the growing sensitivity of many to the unspoken thoughts and feelings of others) humanity will be one vast organism in perfect harmony, and every unit, still thinking itself a unit, will yet feel with every other, giving nevertheless its individual colour to all it takes into its consciousness. Then life will be again real. Humanity is now like a diseased body; it does not work as one. Most people know the history of cancer. Certain cells of the body cease to work for the whole. Working only for themselves they take food in excess, grow and multiply in excess of the bodily needs, and at last reach such a swollen pitch that there is not blood enough for them, and the middle cells die. Thus after casting out these dead ones an open ulcer is formed, and at last the patient dies, worn out with pain, with loss of blood and rest. And with him therefore die the cells who thought to flourish so exuberantly. Therefore every man who works for humanity works for himself, for into that humanity for which he works he is born again and again. Every good thought we plant in another makes his actions better, and these react on his friends, and they through widening circles on all humanity. So when we are again on earth, we find things the better and the pleasanter for that good thought we sowed perhaps ages before. The Oversoul may be likened to a group of men who agree together to become an orchestra. Each with the consent of the others selects a special instrument and goes away to learn it. Each has his difficulties, each produces many false notes, each goes through long and painful practice. No one can complain of these or look down upon another, for the arrangement was signed by all. Since they all learn separate instruments, the tasks and pains of no one resemble those of any other. But though they thus differ, all alike are necessary, for when all are perfect musicians every instrument is as necessary as every other to the perfect harmony of the whole. And as until they are all perfect they cannot play their symphonies, so till all men are perfect we cannot really *live*, as life will be, ages hence. Except by assuming the reality of this one life in us all there is no possible means of accounting for sympathy with pain. Scientifically it is accounted for by the fact that through prehistoric ages of human history, such tribes as could not develop an internal unity of feeling could not oppose a united front to the enemy, and were destroyed as incoherent units by those who at any rate during war had developed the power to act and feel as one. But this is only the statement of the *process* by which those who had the nascent capacity of sympathy survived at the expense of those who had it. We are not as far from the source and cause of origination of sympathy as ever. It is frequently our fate in the study of science to be offered a process instead of a cause. We ask *how* sympathy arises among men. Because those who had it not get slain by *those who had it*, is our answer. It is just this *having it* that remains for explanation. In physical science you can get very fair *description of process*, but of accounts of beginnings and of causes, nothing. Sympathy is self-recognition in another, or better, the self-recognition of the supreme in both. How could one man's pain possibly affect another if they were two really totally distinct beings? No more than a rent in my coat could affect yours. Every feeling of sympathy is absolute proof of one life-spirit in men.

Theosophists are therefore entitled to think that the promulgation of the principles of Theosophy will do much to make the world brighter, to make men use their intellects, to make them unselfish, to make them avoid sin, to make them recognise their responsibility for all they do and think, and for the condition of their fellows. It is of advantage to develop carefully this conception of one all-pervading Life, because it is one which is said to have no practical outcome. And whilst we can truly say that it *has* most vitally important practical bearings, this is alike true of all the Theosophic tenets, however apparently merely aërially mystic. In the meditations of the real Eastern students of mysticism, this subject comes first. They are expected by fixed and constant meditation on this conception of *one* Life in all to come at last actually to realise it, and *then* the selfish personality has its death-blow. It is not a mere metaphysical idea; it is the only guide of life worth having. This being true of *this* conception, it is our duty as Theosophists to enquire closely into the philosophy of Theosophy, and, picking out and learning one by one its more important teachings, to gradually learn their bearing upon daily life. Never think anything in Theosophy unpractical; it all bears on one or another degree of practical life. If we hope to better humanity, we must study its deepest teachings with this view, finding out *how* they are practical and how they can be simplified for popular understanding. But we cannot simplify them till we understand them in their difficult form. Theosophy is new to England, and most of its ideas have no English words. For instance, this One Life with its attributes has no word in English. So we have to study the Theosophic ideas in a somewhat Sanskrit dress, and when this is fully penetrated it is easy for us to translate for beginners. Parabrahm, Jiva, Mahat, Alaya, Buddhi, Atma, cannot be expressed more shortly than by a phrase or even a sentence in English.

Jiva is the one life viewed in its most abstract degree. Atma is the one life as the unmanifest universal soul, before any activity, containing the foreplan of all that will be. In its next stage it is Buddhi, more active than the last. Mahat is its manifestation in the thought of the higher Manas. Kama is its manifestation as the desire for matter or material sensation. Prana is its manifestation as physical vitality. But with all the manifestations there is one common feature, namely consciousness.

It is increasingly maintained by science that there is no consciousness in the cells of our bodies; that there is in them no life different in kind from that which exists in a drop of water; that as we can make two particles of hydrogen unite with one of oxygen to form water, so it is within measurable probability that we shall soon make inorganic elements unite in higher and higher degrees of complexity till at last our compound exhibits life; in fact that life or prana is not a special thing, not conscious, but only a specially complex degree of physical forces, and that all bodily life, all the activity of bodily cells are a question only of chemical, thermic, electrical, and physical forces. But if in reply we say that it is not so, that prana is a special and particular force, that it is in fact the soul of the cell, we must be prepared to say why. On one side is the ordinary physiologist suggesting that as we can make oxygen and hydrogen unite to form water, and as we can make alcohol by a slightly more complex synthesis, and further such a nitrogenised body as quinine, so one day we shall make a speck of protoplasm and find we have a living cell, thus bridging the gulf between organic and inorganic. For it *is* a gulf, and in no wise bridged over by the stepping-stone of *living* protoplasm not yet organised into cells. We say that by combining inorganic matter in any degree of complexity by the aid of any physical forces, you will never get anything but physical forces and matter, never get anything which exhibits life. We appeal to the facts. The *plant* truly can take its nitrogen, oxygen, hydrogen, carbon, etc., in various inorganic combinations and combine them together into living matter that exhibits vitality, *because the plant has already vitality*. There is the old secret. Vitality can add to itself, can call forth life from that in which life is latent, from the unliving molecules of salts and gases, but science is no nearer than a thousand years ago from performing such a piece of alchemy as this.

Science is seeking to build up the above from the below, to combine the physical forces till they reach and become the life-forces, and it *cannot be done*. Physical and chemical forces combined yield only physical and chemical forces again, be they as complex as you please. The idea that because by combining oxygen and hydrogen with an electric spark we can produce water, therefore by combining more numerous elements in greater complexity we shall in time make protoplasm, is false in every particular. The electric spark, the oxygen, and the hydrogen, are enough to produce the water; you do not previously need water. But to produce protoplasm you *do* previously need protoplasm, and it is this which does the work. Secondly there is a distinction between dead and living protoplasm, and there is no distinction between dead and living water. The life of the protoplasm consists in a continuous interstitial balance of construction and destruction, and the mark of its death is the cessation of its constructive activities, and the performance of destruction along different lines. Life is a flow of *constructive energy* arising within the cell, and it *governs* but *is not* the force stored up in the food supplied, which forces can by no process be made to yield phenomena of life. Between living cells (and no form of matter not cellular exhibits life) and all other forms of matter there are no intermediate links, the activities are different in kind, and they cannot come under the same formula. Science is carefully throwing dust in its own eyes by refusing to recognise the hiatus between the vital energy that controls physics—chemical forces, and those forces themselves, however complex. For the exhibition of vitality in newly-formed (daughter cells, buds, etc.) vitality must have previously been present in a similar organism, and it cannot be supplied from any other source. Therefore it is of distinct category. Protoplasm does not exist except as cell-units each with a life of their own. The transition stages between inanimate loose distinct molecules as of water, and the living cells of protoplasm do not exist. And if science is right in its contention that one day we shall produce protoplasm as we do water, they ought to exist. We have no right to *take it for granted* that one day we shall acquire power to do what we cannot as yet see the beginnings of the way to do. Between the soulless disjuncted molecules of chemistry, and the living, purposeful, encolonied cells there is too great a gulf. The cell is organised in itself and in its relations to its fellows; it falls as a bit into the design and collective life of the whole organism, and it has its own work and thought and conscious being. Truly, the life-wave which is now in the physical world exhibiting as physical forces will in time mount to and become the pranic forces of life, but only because those other forces were already there before to help them. By what physico-chemical forces shall we ever hope to make dead flesh live again? Yet what we as physical scientists cannot hope to do, the so-called unconscious cells of our bodies do after every meal. But are these cells unconscious? We have said that it is the leading characteristic of the One Life to become the consciousness on every plane? What is the test of consciousness? We will not try any definitions of our own, but accept one provided for us by Professor Romanes. He says that wherever in the animal and vegetable worlds we see an exhibition of the power of choice, we may infer consciousness. Very well; let us take the physical plane first. Make a saturated solution in boiling water of any salt. For every degree that the solution cools, a new group of molecules precipitates. What determines that some and not the others shall at any moment come out of solution? This no more and no less implies freewill than the act of a child in taking cake instead of bread, but if we infer consciousness in one we ought to in the other. There is no absolute proof for a man of the presence of consciousness anywhere in all being except himself, but the rational attitude is to assume that wherever outside himself he observes an act which in himself, whether volitional or not, is attended with consciousness, such act was conscious.

It is, however, characteristic of the age that an opposite assumption is made, and that an overwhelming majority of the lives in nature are quietly regarded as having their being in unconsciousness. The onus of proof should, however, lie on that side. We are aware that all of our non-instructive actions are preceded by purpose, and irradiated throughout by consciousness, and that they carry out the purpose we design. Whenever, therefore, in any form of being we see similar actions, achieving objects of importance to the life of the organism, the natural inference should be that these also are preceded by purpose and accompanied by consciousness. The scientific course of assuming the usual and probable till the strange and unusual is proved, should be followed here also. And in following it we assume purpose and consciousness, because such accords with the invariable conditions in the only place where we have direct knowledge, namely, ourselves; leaving to the materialist the task of proving the opposite, or of believing the improved unprobable. In passing, one may note that materialism is constantly, almost habitually, employed in assuming as true that which is absolutely opposed to experience, and demanding of its opponents that they shall prove the opposite. We can well afford to decline to be thus cornered. It is a common and empty aphorism of materialistic schools that no thought can occur where there is no brain. Now in declining to prove the opposite, we are entitled to demand proof of the assertion. Brain action is vivid in proportion to the quantity of blood in the skull, provided its flow is healthy. But in sleep, when the blood-flow is at its minimum, thought and imagination are often marvellous in their vividity. This thought and imagery are not transacted by the brain, and often barely reach the brain-memory at all. Under some anæsthetics, the whole personality, thinking and observing, is sometimes absolutely outside the body, and has the body as an object beside it. These experiences of sleep and anæsthesia are sufficient to afford *à priori* ground for holding that thought *can* go on without a brain, and who says the opposite should prove it. Brain does *not* vary with mind. The brain of a new-born infant compared with that of an adult has not the ratio of development which obtains between that of an infant and that of an adult. They grow quite out of ratio. At the other end of life it is the same. An aged body, rigid and calcified arteries and deadened senses, may go with a brilliant and stately intellect as mobile as that of a man of forty. In other words the brain has a cycle of growth and death that has only a limited correspondence with that of mind. To students of occultism the problem ceases altogether, for they *know* that mind properly trained may be made absolutely independent of brain. It may be granted that in the usual case a thought is accompanied by a physical change of molecular configuration and a passage of a nerve-current from cells to cells, but what molecular or cellular configuration can be regarded as accompanying the sense of self-identity that is at the back of every conscious state? To say that such configuration is conceivable, is an accompaniment of the sense of self-identity, of the ideas of time and space, or of any abstract idea, is to use words that are entirely innocent of meaning.

It may perhaps now be clear what we mean by saying that One Life on seven planes pervades the universe, and that on every plane it shews itself in a different way. The forces of the physical plane cannot by any combination be made to rise to the pranic plane. They can only do so under the influence of prana which in living cells is already on that plane. Vitality, prana, in its turn cannot become desire, Kama, cannot rise to the Kamic plane of itself unless it enter or be controlled by an organism which has already Kama. And so all the way up. The forces of each plane rise to the next plane only under the influence of forces already there. Always the lower tending more completely to pass under the sway of the higher. And within ourselves, if we had not within us the divine light of our higher egos as stimulus and ideal, we could get no higher than our own fourth plane, the plane of reason; for no reasoning or combination of reasons (the fourth plane of conscious life) could make us spiritual on the fifth or Higher Manasic plane unless the Higher Manas were already on that plane to help. Reason might afford a *negative* morality, an avoidance of crime, and even a sort of benevolence, but it would be limited to the individual and to selfishness as a basis. True altruism is a feeling, a desire for the welfare of others without any regard for one's own welfare at all: whilst that altruism which was simply an accumulated heredity aided by natural selection finds its basis all the way along in personal considerations and could never transcend these. No reasoning could make a man *yearn* for the welfare of others, which is *positive* altruism.

Absolute Spirit at the dawn of the universe descends into matter, being *therein* at first unconscious, conscious only on its own, the highest, divinest plane. Passing lightly and subconsciously through the downward steps of intervening consciousness, it finds itself at last fully awake in matter, and then begins its slow ascent, retracing the steps upon which formerly it came down, and making itself on the upsteps fully conscious where on the down it had been nearly unconscious, yet making use on the way up of the next higher landmark which on the way down it had traced out for itself, such landmarks being foreplans or forefigurings and outlines and ideals serving as stimuli to make them real and vivid on the up-path.

HERBERT CORYN.

CPSIA information can be obtained
at www.ICGtesting.com
Printed in the USA
LVIC061221030520
654917LV00020B/939